HUMOR

By
Charles S. Hellman and Robert A. Tiritilli

Copyright 2013

ALL RIGHT RESERVED
39844 Somerset Ave.
Palm Desert, CA 92211
www.LuckySports.net

All rights reserved. Do not duplicate or redistribute in any form. All contents of this book including the concept, elements of design and layout, graphic images and elements, unless otherwise noted, is copyrighted material and protected by trade and other laws and may not be copied or imitated in whole or in part. Violators will be prosecuted to the maximum extent possible. No logo, graphic, character or caption from any page may be copied or retransmitted unless expressly permitted in writing by LuckySports$_{TM}$. Any rights not expressly granted herein are reserved.

ISBN 0-935938-44-9
Illustrations by Robert A. Tiritilli
Cover & Interior Design by Charles S. Hellman
Edited by Charles S. Hellman

"Sorry... this is NOT a hotel!"

 **Eskimo kiss**

 **Longshot**

 **Future jockey**

 **Big bettor**

"I'm so hungry... I could eat a horse!"

"You'll be OK... you're just a little horse!"

Good Weight Horse

Always look a *GIFTED* horse in the mouth!

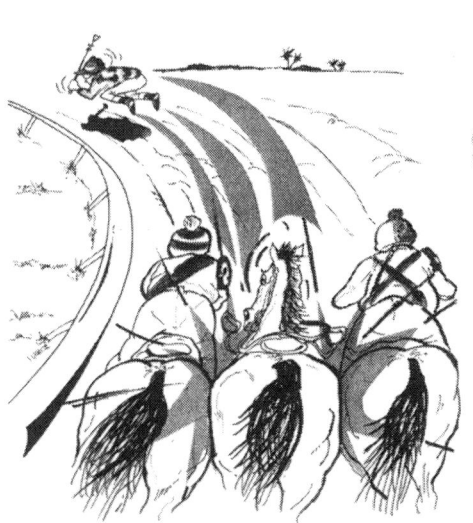

"I feel naked without my saddle!"

Gone Hollywood

Jockey's jockey

Good BOX horse

"I'm looking for a STAAABLE man!"

Tough day at the track

Coupled

Jockey error

Under restraint

"No... you can't bet your shirt!"

"No... you can't go POTTY, now?"

And quit calling me HORSE-FACE!"

"What a price you paid!"

First time starter

"Go faster... over!"

Sowing his *Wild Oats*

enLIGHTENment

"Even the glue factory rejected him!"

Looks *fast*

End of the rope

"Looks like a bookie's betting notes!"

"Not to worry... Life is *SHORT*."

"We're lucky, in the old days...
they would shoot you!"

Using a battery

Sleeper

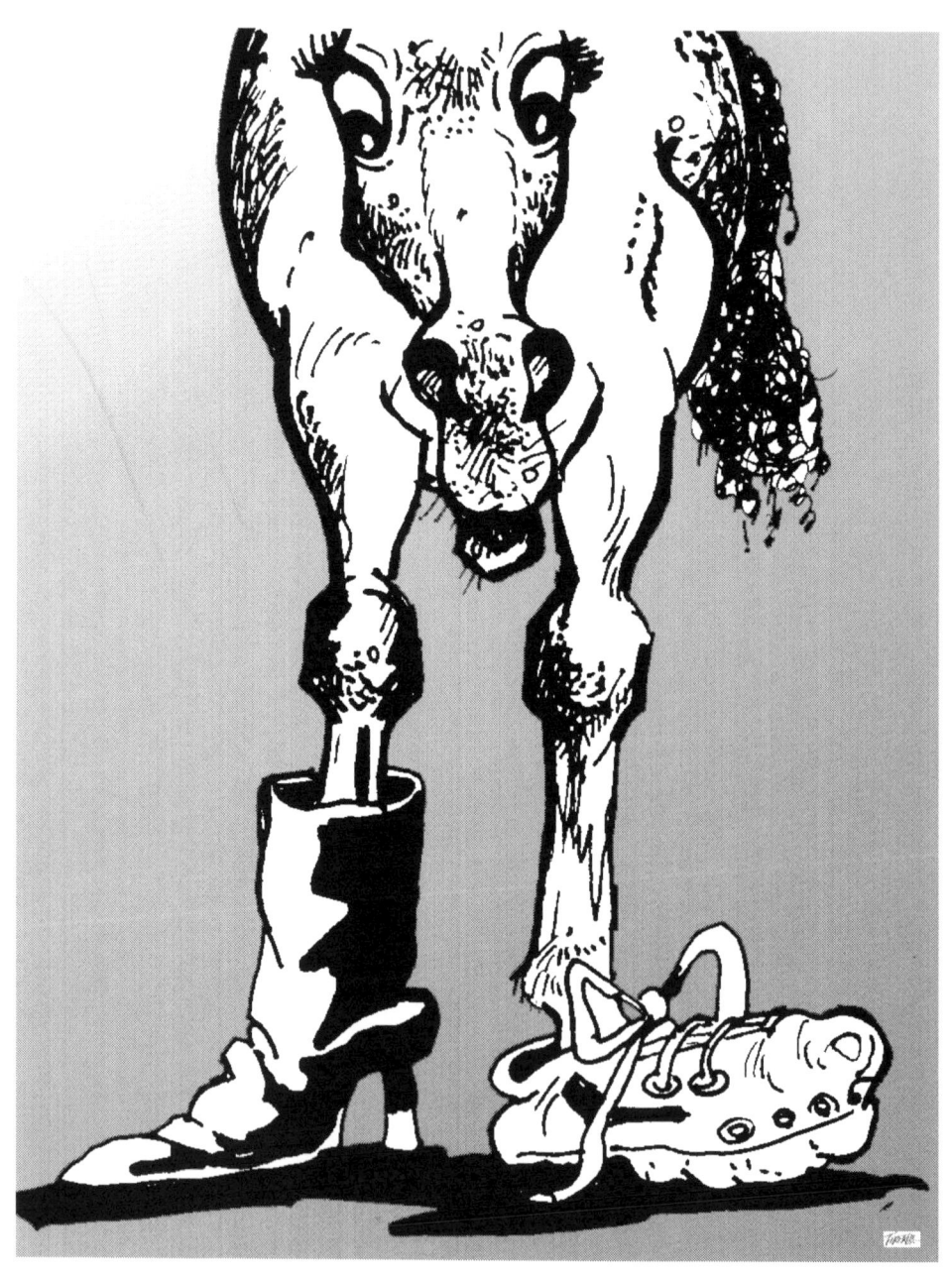

New shoes

Good horseman

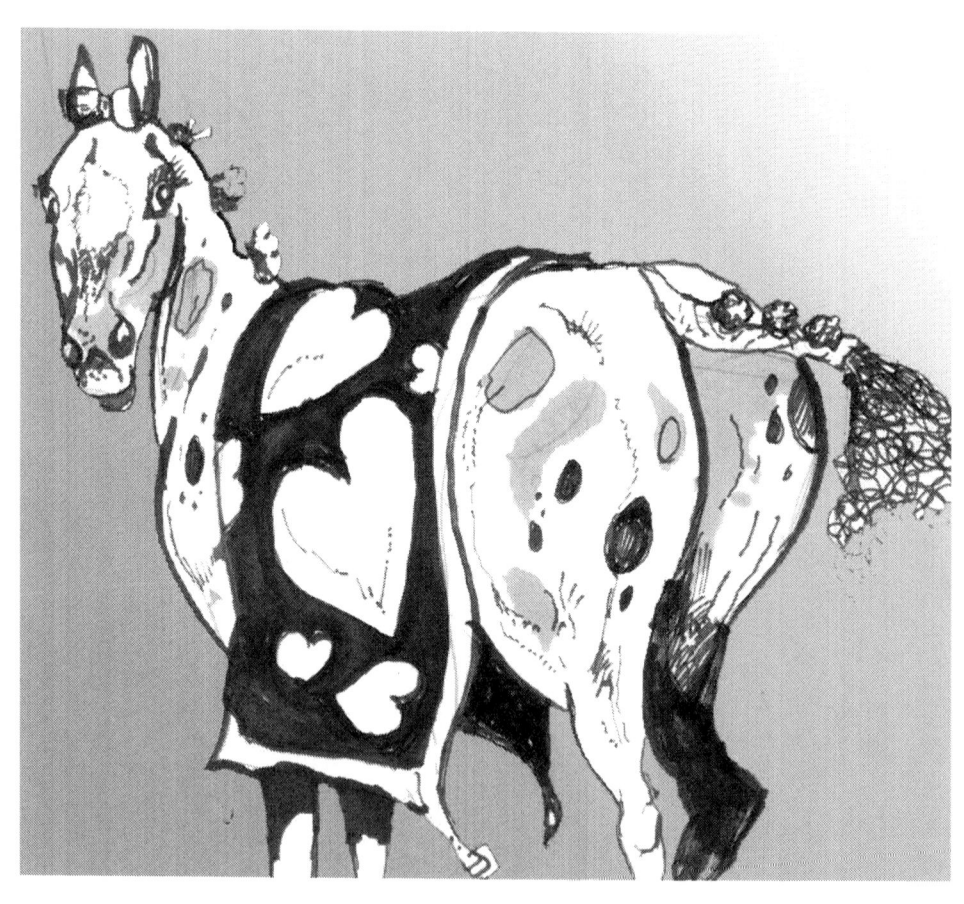

"Does this blanket make my ass look TOO FAT?"

Horse Greedey tells jockey where to GO!

Horse Fly

Printed in Great Britain
by Amazon